COLLECT-A-PET READER

My cute
RaBBIt

Written by Helen Anderton

make
believe
ideas

Reading together

This book is an ideal first reader for your child, combining simple words and sentences with beautiful photography of rabbits. Here are some of the many ways you can help your child with their early steps in reading.

Encourage your child to:

- Look at and explore the detail in the pictures.
- Sound out the letters in each word.
- Read and repeat each short sentence.

Look at the pictures

Make the most of each page by talking about the pictures and spotting key words. Here are some questions you can use to discuss each page as you go along:

- Do you like this rabbit?
- If so, what do you like about it?
- What would it feel like to touch?
- How would you look after it?

Look at rhymes

Many of the sentences in this book are simple rhymes. Encourage your child to recognise rhyming words. Try asking the following questions:

- What does this word say?
- Can you find a word that rhymes with it?
- Look at the ending of two words that rhyme. Are they spelt the same? For example, "hay" and "day", "eyes" and "size".

Test understanding

It is one thing to understand the meaning of individual words, but you need to check that your child understands the facts in the text.

- Play "spot the mistake". Read the text as your child looks at the words with you, but make an obvious mistake to see if he or she has understood. Ask your child to correct you and provide the right word.
- After reading the facts, shut the book and make up questions to ask your child.
- Ask your child whether a fact is true or false.
- Provide your child with three answers to a question and ask him or her to pick the correct one.

Rabbit quiz

At the end of the book, there is a simple quiz. Ask the questions and see if your child can remember the right answers from the text. If not, encourage him or her to look up the answers.

Key words

These pages provide practice with very common words used in the context of the book. Read the sentences with your child and encourage him or her to make up more sentences using the key words listed around the border.

Picture dictionary

A picture dictionary page illustrates the things you need when looking after a rabbit.

Watch me grow

Just look at me! I'm very small.
I can't see anything at all.
Soon, I'll open both my eyes,
and grow to be the perfect size.

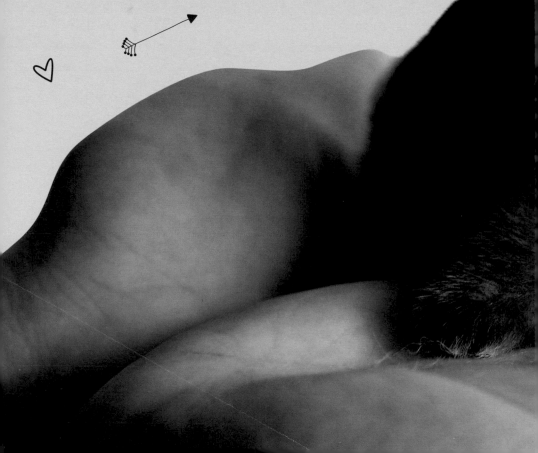

DID YOU KNOW?
Rabbits don't open their eyes until they are about ten days old.

eye

nose

5

Run and jump

My little legs are very strong.
I use them when I hop along.
Watch me take a great big jump
and land with an almighty thump!

leg

DID YOU KNOW?

Rabbits have very strong legs. They can run at speeds of 80 km/h (50 mph).

Look at my ears!

I have a pair of fluffy ears.
They keep me cool and let me hear.
Stroke my ears from time to time.
Whose are longer – yours or mine?

DID YOU KNOW?

Rabbits have very long ears. This gives them excellent hearing.

ear

Time to eat

My favourite meal is grass or hay,
so give some to me every day.
When I am good, give me a treat
of yummy vegetables to eat!

carrot

DID YOU KNOW?
Rabbits are herbivores,
which means that they
do not eat meat.

hay

My sharp teeth

I have sharper teeth than you.
They help me bite and help me chew.
Eating hay keeps my teeth strong
and stops them getting way too long!

whiskers

DID YOU KNOW?
A rabbit's teeth grow constantly, but they are worn down by chewing.

tooth

Dig, dig, dig!

Digging with my two front paws
is so much fun when I'm outdoors.
I make a hole and jump inside –
the perfect place for me to hide!

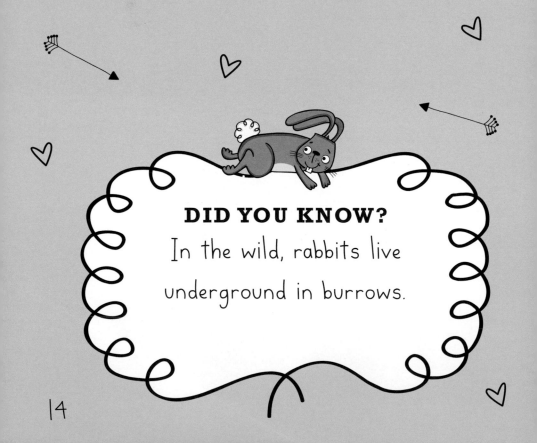

DID YOU KNOW?
In the wild, rabbits live
underground in burrows.

burrow

Play with me

Do you want to play with me?
I've got a lot of energy!
Give me toys that I can chew,
paper tubes and boxes, too!

paper tube

DID YOU KNOW?

You can make chewable toys
for your rabbit out of
newspaper or cardboard.

toy

Grooming

My fur is long and soft to touch.
It keeps me warm out in my hutch.
Groom my coat when you have time,
so I stay clean and looking fine!

soft fur

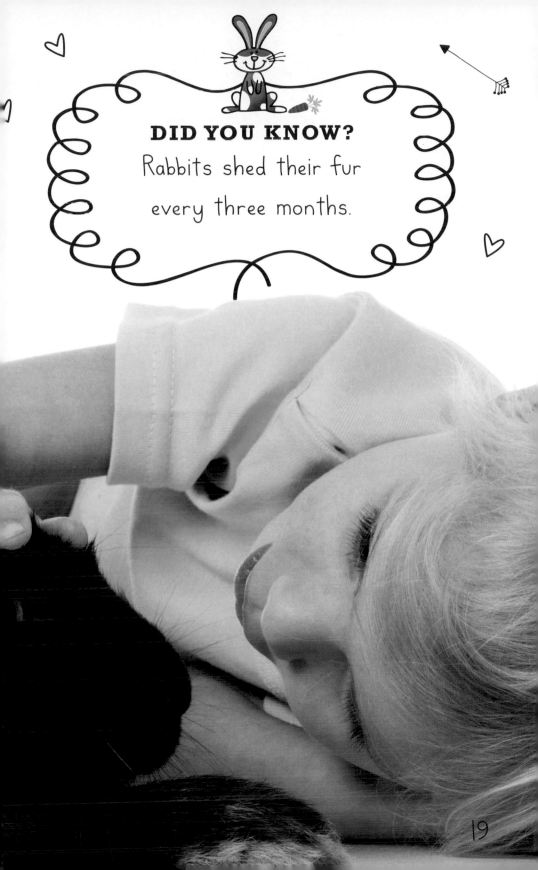

DID YOU KNOW?

Rabbits shed their fur
every three months.

19

What's that sound?

When I hear a strange new sound,
I thump my feet upon the ground.
I get scared quite easily,
so make sure you look after me!

foot

DID YOU KNOW?

When they are scared, rabbits thump their feet to warn other rabbits of danger.

At the vet

We're going to see the vet today.
I'd rather stay indoors and play!
She will make sure I'm not ill –
if she can get me to sit still!

DID YOU KNOW?
Rabbits should visit a vet
at least once a year.

vet

23

Showjumping

I like to jump up very high,
so I can almost touch the sky.
Enter me into a race
and I'll be sure to come first place!

DID YOU KNOW?

Rabbits can compete in
showjumping competitions,
just like horses!

Zzzzzz!

It's time to have a little nap
inside my hutch or on your lap.
I'm as happy as can be
because you take good care of me!

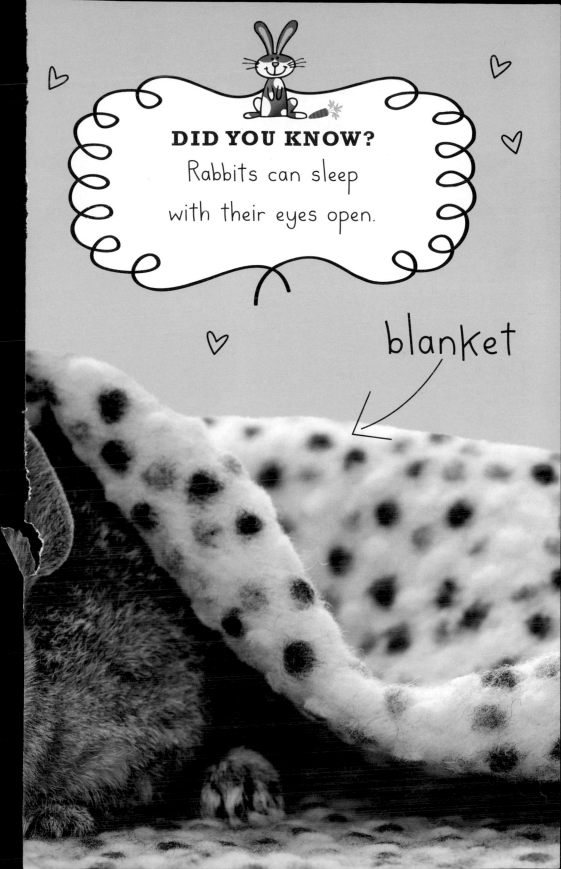

DID YOU KNOW?

Rabbits can sleep
with their eyes open.

blanket

Rabbit quiz

How much do you know about me?

1. At what age do rabbits open their eyes?

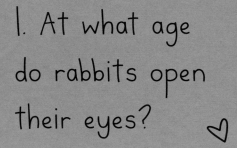

They open their eyes at about ten days old.

2. How often do rabbits shed their fur?

They shed their fur every three months.

3. Can rabbits sleep with their eyes open?

Yes.

4. Where do rabbits live in the wild?

They live underground in burrows.

5. How do rabbits wear down their teeth? ♡

♡

They wear down their teeth by chewing

6. How often should rabbits visit the vet?

♡
♡

They should visit the vet at least once a year.

7. Do rabbits eat meat?

♡
♡

No.

I ♥ up ♥ look ♥ we ♥ like ♥ and

yes ♥

it ♥

see ♥

she ♥

me ♥

of ♥

in ♥

come ♥

Key words

Here are some key words used in context. Help your child to use other words from the border in simple sentences.

I can jump **very** high.

Look **at** my tail!

♥ don't ♥ am ♥ all ♥ to ♥ my ♥ ge

I live in **a** hutch.

I **don't** eat meat.

My fur **is** soft.

Can **you** see my whiskers?

Picture dictionary

box

brush

burrow

hay

hutch

toy

treat

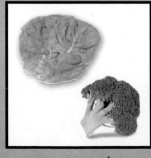

vegetables

vet